FAILURE

MARC BLAKE

Crombie Jardine
PUBLISHING LIMITED
www.crombiejardine.com

This edition was first published by
Crombie Jardine Publishing Limited in 2006

ISBN 1-905102-76-3

Written by Marc Blake
Cover design by Stewart Ferris

Printed and bound in the United Kingdom by
William Clowes Ltd, Beccles, Suffolk

CONTENTS

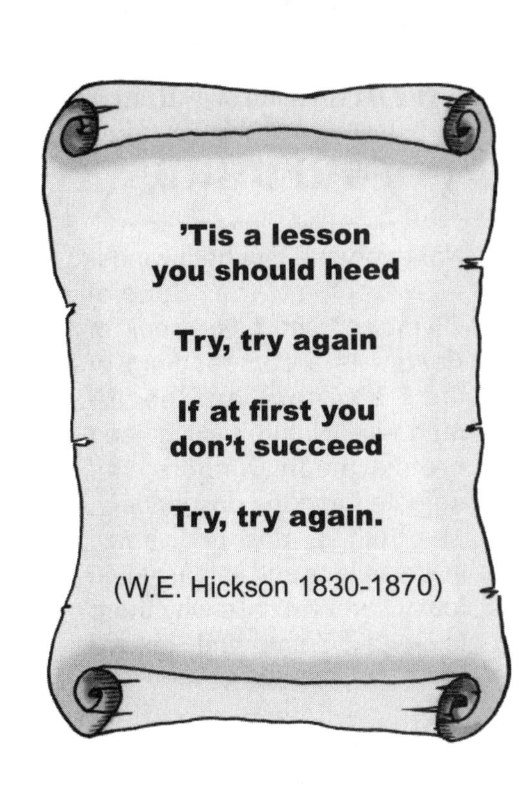
'Tis a lesson
you should heed
Try, try again
If at first you
don't succeed
Try, try again.
(W.E. Hickson 1830-1870)

FOREWORD

Not everyone can be a winner – except at the Special Olympics. *The Little Book of Failure* is a compendium of life's also-rans and never-made-its. Nature's silver and bronze medal winners, the defeated and the despondent. The truth is, *most people fail*: in life, in love and in that stupid lousy career. That's why there is Donald Trump and Richard

Branson and then there is wage-slave scum like the rest of us. There are rich lists everywhere, but what about the poor? Where are those unique riches to rags stories? What about those who had it all and pissed it away? Or never got there in the first place? It's time to mutter the truth:

'Succeeders need underachievers to make them look good!'

SEVEN SPINS ON FAILURE

Failure is...
only deferred success

Failure is...
confirmation that it was never going to work anyway

Failure is...
being in a bigger team than the winners

Failure is...
historically inevitable

Failure is...
God's fault. After all, who made the duck-billed platypus?

Failure is...
nature's way of keeping it real

Failure is...
proof that you took part

FICTIONAL FAILURE ICONS

Bart
(underachiever and proud of it!)

Homer

Joey Tribiani

Basil Fawlty

David Brent

Rupert Pupkin
(King of Comedy)

Holden Caulfield
(Catcher in the Rye)

Hancock

Inspector Clouseau

Don Quixote

Dougal, Droopy, Snoopy, Scooby...
all cartoon dogs

YOU ARE FAILING IN YOUR JOB WHEN...

...you have stars on your shirt – not on the review of your latest movie.

...you receive no email, not even on the intranet. Not even Spam.

...you receive a get well soon card from your colleagues and you haven't been ill.

...your workstation doubles as the cleaner's cupboard.

...you escape a mass downsizing because no one knew you still worked here.

...you are charged with sexual harassment only to have it laughed out of court.

...you call in sick and the boss says 'OK. Take another day...no, the week.'

...you make up a fantastic excuse for being 15 minutes late and no one cares.

...19 year olds are promoted above your head.

...and you are the boss's nephew.

FAILURE QUOTE

When Thomas Edison tried 999 ways to make a light bulb he was asked, **'Are you going to have a thousand failures?'**

His reply: **'I didn't fail. I just discovered another way not to invent the electric light bulb.'**

FAILURE ICON #1
VINCENT VAN GOGH

Vincent Van Gogh had two unhappy romances in England and failed as a clerk, art salesman and preacher in Belgium where he was fired for being too keen. In Belgium? He lived on donations from his brother Theo for the rest of his life. In Paris he painted all day and night until his health was

ruined. He moved to the South of France hoping that his artist friends would join him and create an art school. They didn't. Only Gauguin came and Vincent went after him with a razor. Vincent later cut off his own left earlobe. He seesawed between madness and sanity until he was committed to an asylum in Saint-Remy. In 1890 he was released into the care of Dr Gatchet but two months later shot himself "for the good of all". He sold just one painting. Top failure.

FAILURE FACT

Enter the words 'miserable failure' on the search engine Google and it comes up with... **George W Bush**.

This happened because a group of web developers attached the term "miserable failure" to a link to a George Bush online biography.

The practice of attaching cheeky links in this way is known as ‘Google bombing’.

Adam Mathes, a web logger, is credited with inventing the practice in 2001.

George W Bush is currently still in office at the time of writing.

...THIS BLOODY THING WON'T ... PRODUCTS THAT FAILED

Betamax

Although vastly superior to VHS it lost the video battle of the 1980's (the great failed decade). File with **Laserdisc** and **8 track** (in car stereo for tank-owners).

The Sinclair C5

An electric car that goes as far as the flex will permit...and then tumbles over. Nice work Sir Clive. See also **The Skoda**. Russian junk on wheels. Now bizarrely popular again – amongst pedestrians.

The Puffball Skirt

1986 was a year when women wanted to look like a pumpkin or a Panto dame. OK, all right, it was just the Duchess of Pork and Pepsi & Shirley ...see also **batwing sleeves**. Gahhh.

The Space Pen

Why do you need to write a letter in orbit? In space no one can hear your pen leaking. Also see the **divers watch**. "Ooh - just what I need - a stopwatch while I'm underwater. Cool. I am drowning in twenty three sec...glug."

The Spork

It's a spoon, it's a fork. It doesn't hold soup and it can't spear food. It's in the bin. Also the **Plastic Stirrer.**

It's not fucking cutlery – it's the loose bits off an airfix kit. Let's be clear here. The Chinese only got as far as chopsticks. We ain't about to go back there.

The Illuminating Pepper Grinder

Why do we need to light up a condiment? Contains batteries so heavy that the bottom half of grinder falls in your pasta. Teams up with **over elaborate bottle openers**. You have been given one at Christmas

every year for the last five years. You still use the simple waiter's friend don't you? Shit on a metal stick.

The Breville Cheese Toastie Maker

Ideal for those who like their sandwich filling at the temperature of molten magma. This snack of boiling cheese drips all over counter, your hands and your face.

Nylon

and all artificial fabrics.
E.g. **Terylene, Crimplene**.

How *not* to be fire retardant. Man-made fibres are nowadays consigned to B&B bedsheets. On the positive side, nylon sports garments could be a way of harnessing Chavs to power the national grid.

The Automatic Pet Feeder

Leave kitty home alone. Pet feeder opens. Kitty spreads food and hair over mechanism,

which jams. Kitty waits for next feed. It fails to open. Kitty goes feral and tears open feeder, then goes after sparrows, squirrels, next door's dog and *you* when you get home, you – you feline hating bastard scum.

The Millennium Dome
Commissioned by Tories, screwed up by Labour. We don't need no education. A white elephant six years on and still counting.

DOOM YOUR CHILD... TOP TEN FAILURE NAMES

Keith
Kevin
Clive
Hilary
Brian
Gazza
Nigel
Colin
Vinnie
Ian

Dawn
Michelle
Tracey
Kayleigh
Edwina
Shazza
Myra
Hilary
Patricia
Cruz

FAILURE ICON #2
GUY FAWKES

In 1605 Catholic extremist **Guido Fawkes** and a gang of conspirators plotted to kill King James I and wipe out the British government. However, one of them had a mate in the Houses of Parliament and sent him a letter warning him to stay away on the day of the attack. The letter was intercepted and given to the king. Meanwhile, Guy Fawkes and friends rolled 36

barrels of gunpowder into the cellars of the Houses of Parliament. Guards broke in and arrested them. After four days of torture Guy spilled the beans. He and the plotters were tried for treason; hung, drawn and cut into quarters and their heads were stuck on poles as a warning. The 'Bone fire' tradition started up the next November - but not in memory of the gunpowder plot. It was an effigy of the Pope that was burned.

It wasn't until 200 years later that they changed it to Fawkes.

THIS ISN'T GOING TO WORK!

...WHEN YOU ABSOLUTELY KNOW THAT FAILURE IS ON ITS WAY

"Should this be attached to anything?"

"Is that your wife at the door?"

"No, no, no. The decimal point goes here."

"What happens if I do...this?"

"When you said 'casual' I thought you meant..."

"Yes officer. I've had a drink. So what?"

"Even if you *did* give me the award I'd tell you where to stick it..."

"You haven't pressed 'send' have you?"

"I thought it was dead already..."

FAILURE QUOTE

“A minute’s success pays the failure of years.”

Robert Browning

HOW TO FAIL IN... POLITICS

1.

Tell the truth.

2.

Do not attend public school or a reputable University. Do not study economics, politics or history: instead try air guitar or horticulture.

3.

Ensure you are not on the board of any FTSE companies and have no useful contacts in the military or oil-producing countries.

4.

Marry a woman who cannot and will not keep her trap shut.

5.

As local councillor, conduct surgeries where you make outrageous promises to impressionable young hacks. Renege on them.

6.

Swear allegiance to the party and believe them when they send you to a far flung constituency for 'strategic' purposes.

7.

Unrelentingly question the shameless vote-grabbing policies of party leaders and undermine them with proof of error and/or lies.

8.

...Which you then mention carelessly to journalists because they were nice and bought you a drink.

9.

Cultivate a media profile as an unthinking toff who cares little for the concerns of the proles or helps asylum seekers into the country.

10.

Do not deny, obfuscate or filibuster. Titillate the 4th Estate with "that's for me to know and you to find out".

HOW TO FAIL IN... SPORTS

1.

In pre-teen years cultivate a love of TV and darkened rooms.

2.

Eschew groups where people are being 'picked'.

3.

Subsist on a diet of carbo-hydrate, fags and psychotropic substances. Never 'jog' except for a six pack... of lager.

4.

Do not be trained by Lennox Lewis, rather Lemmy of Motorhead.

5.

Cultivate a losing attitude. Accept that it's 'only a game' and that there is always another match.

6.

If you must play a competitive sport, choose one with weapons such as hockey, baseball or cricket. Then be belligerent on the field.

7.

Ensure all equipment is poorly maintained.

8.

Refuse to shower with other men or to engage in sexual congress with hookers while they look on.

9.

Renege on any sponsor by disgracing their product or be seen promoting a rival item.

10.

Piss away any chance of success with an argumentative and difficult attitude towards managers, coaches, team mates, referees, drug testers, customs officials, paparazzi, Olympic selection committees and clothing or footwear manufacturers. Advertise grills.

FAILED PLANET... PLUTO

Discovered in 1930 – the last planet in our solar system – by Clyde Tombaugh, an American Scientist. Pluto is the Roman god of the underworld. All the other Planets have a proud heritage. Earth is our home; Mercury the winged messenger; Mars the god of war; Venus, goddess of love; Jupiter has its moons; Saturn its rings.

Neptune is the ruler of the sea and Uranus is a cheap bottom gag. Pluto is still better known as the stupid cartoon dog and all cartoon dogs are failures.

FOOT IN MOUTH!

"Drill for oil? You mean drill into the ground to find oil? You're crazy."

Response to Edwin L. Drake's plan in 1859.

"Heavier than air machines are impossible."

Lord Kelvin, 1899.

"Everything that can be invented has been invented."

Charles H Duell
Commissioner, US Office of Patents, 1899.

"Who the hell wants to hear actors talk?"

H.M Warner on the advent of talkies, 1927.

"There's no likelihood that man will ever tap the power of the atom."

Robert Millikan, Nobel Physics prize-winner, 1923.

"Stocks have reached what looks like a permanently high plateau."

Irving Fisher, Professor of Economics, Yale, 1929.

"I think there is a world market for maybe five computers."

Thomas J Watson
IBM chairman, 1943.

"We don't like their sound and guitar music is on the way out."

Decca Records rejecting The Beatles, 1962.

"640K ought to be enough for anybody."

Bill Gates, 1981.

"Results! I have gotten a lot of results. I know several things that won't work."

Thomas Edison.

GOD'S FAILURES EXTINCT ANIMALS AND BIRDS

Dinosaurs
Sabre-toothed tigers
Tasmanian Devils
Moas
Woolly mammoths
Dodos
Great auk
Sea mink

...THIS BLOODY THING WON'T ... MORE PRODUCTS THAT FAIL

X-ray Specs

They don't see through walls. They don't see through women's clothing. They don't help your vision. Pointless.

Leaf Blowers

Let's arrange the leaves in a different pattern, or perhaps all

over our neighbour's garden. OK…I know, let's chase the leaves around while we *blow dry* them.

Hotel Kettles

Unplug kettle. Fill with one cup of water. Plug in. Flick switch. Write a novel. Flick switch up and down. Unplug kettle. Pour out half the water. Repeat. Don't even mention the UHT milk 'pots', the mini sugar pillows or the Corby trouser press.

Family Name Histories

Arrogance expressed as provenance. How fascinating? You were a farmer /blacksmith/ Cleopatra? No one gives a shit you useless streak of piss.

Facial Muscle Toners

I know. I'll shock myself into being beautiful. EST for the FACE that ought to do it… or make me look like Gary Glitter up on another paedo charge.

The Foot Spa

Never used more than once. Anyone can put their feet in a bowl of warm water. If you want bubbles then fart in the bath.

Sat Nav

Another woman giving directions? I don't think so. Most stolen item these days. Now tell me where you are, Sat Nav? Oh, a lock-up in Catford.

THAT LOOKS SHIT
FASHION FAILURES

The Button Fly

In the 1960s, worn on the outside. In the 1990s, still impossible to undo. Lee jeans – the only men who buy your product have shredded fingers and piss-stained underwear. That is why you are going bust.

The Safari Suit

Are you hunting, fishing or shooting? No. You are hanging about in a bar thinking you are Roger Moore. With too many pockets. Went the way of the cravat.

Crochet

Woollen stuff with too many holes in it. Scratchy, uncomfortable. Holey and wholly unflattering. Knitted by grannies for morons or Christians or Christian morons.

Paper Clothing

Another 1960s fad. Paper clothes are now only ever worn in hospital. Uncomfortable *and* a fire hazard. Paper underwear. That's like wrapping yourself in loo roll. Edible underwear – no one wants to eat your soiled encrusted chuddies.

Unisex

His and hers jeans, tank tops, sweatshirts, Afghan coats and – mmm – dungarees. We are not children's presenters.

There are two sexes for a reason. Procreation. This will not happen to anyone wearing unisex clothing.

FAILURE ICON #3
GEORGE BEST

'The first 27 years were sheer bliss and the last 27 have been a disaster.'

Had it all – then pissed it away. **George Best** ensured that Manchester United topped the First Division in 1965 and 1967 and won the European Cup in 1968 (he was European Footballer of the Year). Best scored 178 goals and won 37 caps for Northern Ireland.

Asked what happened to all the money he had earned, Best replied: “I spent a lot on booze, birds and fast cars. The rest I just squandered.” His playboy lifestyle degenerated into alcoholism, bankruptcy, domestic abuse, a prison sentence for drink-driving, and a liver transplant. He was divorced twice and became regular tabloid fodder. He never competed in a World Cup tournament and spent his later years playing for lower league clubs in the UK (Bournemouth)

and in the USA (Fort Lauderdale Strikers).

In 2000 he was diagnosed with liver damage. A year later he was treated for pneumonia and was given anti-alcohol implants. In 2002 he underwent a liver transplant but continued to drink. In November 2005 his internal organs gave out. His Belfast funeral attracted many sporting greats and other drunks.

PATRON SAINTS OF FAILURE

St Jude
– Patron Saint of hopeless causes

St Osmund
– Patron saint of people afflicted by insanity

St Barbara
– Patron saint of people in danger of sudden death

HOW TO FAIL IN...
JOB INTERVIEWS

1.

Dress appropriately – sportswear, smart casual drag, fancy dress – whatever makes you feel comfortable. Alternatively, a merkin or anything vulcanised will send most HR people scurrying to their lickle files.

2.

Ensure that your CV exposes your hobbies (walking and socialising) for what they are – thinly veiled excuses for alcoholism.

3.

On no account be on time. Early or late is good. Preposterously late is better accompanied with a lame excuse. There was a special on at ASDA.

4.

Do not fall into the trap of batting back questions like "And what would you say are your weaknesses?" Confront them head on. "I am unreliable and grossly incompetent – but I consider them strengths here at BT."

5.

Leer at the embonpoint of any female present. Talk to cleavage and make it your friend. Get whiplash at the sound of stilettos.

6.

Embroider your gap year with interesting titbits: "I never made India. Missed the ferry. Went back to mum's and got smashed on skunk for a year. Same difference but without the dysentery, eh? You Indian then?"

7.

Explain absences in your CV with tales of amnesia, repressed memory and hints at detox.

8.

Act like you have the job already! When can I start? How about right now. Have you got a list of employees I can harrass?

9.

Be tactful of the differently-abled. So who's the Stephen Hawking next door? No, the mong. Is that a quota thing?

10.

Physical contact is always memorable. Try a firm handshake, a back slap and a snog for good measure.

HOW TO FAIL IN... BUSINESS

1.

Do not make a business plan. Instead rely on psychics and the advice of relatives; themselves utter failures in business so they know the terrain.

2.

Do not research the market. If your product is good enough it will create a market – e.g. Tuna ice cream, Scrotal clippers.

3.

Find a partner to match your skills. If you lack planning and bookkeeping skills find someone equally flaky and flamboyant. Live the dream until the Bailiffs arrive.

4.

Don't keep records of transactions. Cash is good, liquid is good and the VAT people are always good for a bribe.

5.

Drop the VAT people a line but don't bother with those tricky quarterly forms.

6.

Find an accountant in the pub; someone who knows or who claims to know how best to stash it all away from the taxman – ideally offshore, somewhere like the Isle of Wight, which is a tax haven.

7.

Impress your suppliers with late deliveries of stock. Then their customers will want your product even more!

8.

Keep Customer Service to a minimum. A surly greeting is good, along with a lack of knowledge about the product, along with blaming management (see BT or HomeBase).

9.

Have an automated answering service; this is the quickest way of losing business. "Press three for some automated cunt."

10.
Go into business with your brother-in-law.

FAILED SMOKER

Rodrigo de Jerez, one of Columbus' fellow explorers, was the first European to smoke tobacco. He was arrested and thrown into prison for lighting up in public.

FAILED ASSASSIN

Johann Georg Elser was the first of many who tried to kill Hitler.

On the 8th November 1939 he hid in a broom cupboard in the Bürgerbräukeller near where the Fuhrer was due to make a speech. In attendance were

Goebbels, Ribbentrop and Himmler.

Hitler gave the speech, finishing at 9:10. The bomb went off at 9:20, bringing down the ceiling and killing eight First World War veterans, a waitress and injuring more than sixty people.

The result was that Hitler received even more sympathy for his mission to purify Germany. Elser was caught, tried and died at Dachau in 1945.

FAILED ASTRONAUT

Michael Collins was the third man on the Apollo 11 space flight. While Edwin 'Buzz' Aldrin deserves a failure accolade for being the second man to step onto the surface of the moon, Mike remained up in the capsule orbiting the earth with his space pen.

HOW TO FAIL AT...
HUSBANDRY

1.

Pick someone who you find attractive only when legless and take them up the aisle before sobriety rears it's splitting head.

2.

Ensure the honeymoon is booked in a place that is likely to engender memories of lost luggage, malaria, political turmoil & Act of God.

3.

Always be on the lookout for sexual alternatives to your spouse and leap at every chance, from shopgirls to needy MILT's and MILF's.

4.

On no account listen to her whinging demands to 'have a talk'.

5.

Forget every birthday and anniversary. If you must provide a gift let it be purchased from an all-night

garage. Briquettes or Anti Freeze are ideal last minute solutions as are flowers that were once tied to a railing.

6.

Cultivate outdoor hobbies such as sports, ornithology and dogging.

7.

Make unreasonable sexual demands of your partner, involving third parties and coprophilia.

8.

Get friends to leave mysterious texts and emails, to slam down phones and to engineer flimsy excuses for your continued overnight absences.

9.

Have her sister, brother or mother.

10.

Insult every member of her family in ingenious and actionable ways.

FOR EVERY JONATHAN... NOT SO FAMOUS SIBLINGS

Paul Ross
Mark Thatcher
Terry Major-Ball
Michael Attenborough
Emilio Estevez
Beau Bridges
Steven, William and Daniel Baldwin
Eric Roberts

HOW TO FAIL AT... PARENTING

1.

Do not be present at the birth, or even at the conception.

2.

Refer to the child as 'it' and refuse all attempts at gender stereotyping.

3.

Ensure that the mother is on a steady drip of hard spirits and crack whilst breastfeeding.

4.

At birth, put the child's name down for the local sink school.

5.

Have it raised by a succession of governesses, nannies and au pairs with no knowledge of English, but a good knowledge of blokes named Keith.

6.

Ignore blatant cries for attention. If it wants to eat it will discover how to use a can opener for itself.

7.

Allow the child to build up a strong immune system by permitting it to crawl about in challenging environments: E.g. beer gardens, communal changing rooms or near the dog waste bin in parks.

8.

Conduct loud arguments with your spouse concerning the

child's inevitable future as a junkie/Ho/HomeBase employee – just like its mother!

9.

Do not lock any cupboards, especially those containing household items such as bleach, sharp knives and power tools.

10.

Give it a name that will ensure maximum bullying and embarrassment such as Nobby, Dick, Fanny or Keith.

FAILED ASSASSIN #2

John Hinckley Jr saw the film *Taxi Driver* fifteen times before enrolling in a Yale writing course to be near the actress Jodie Foster. He left poems in her mailbox and believed that assassinating a President would gain her love.

Hinckley went to one of President Carter's campaign appearances, but left his gun collection in his hotel room.

In March 1981 he wrote a letter to Jodie about his plan to assassinate President Reagan. At a public event he stepped from a crowd of reporters and fired six shots. The bullets hit Reagan in the chest, Press Secretary James Brady in the temple, Officer Thomas Delahanty in the neck, and

Security Agent Timothy J. McCarthy in the stomach.

Hinckley was arrested and found not guilty by reason of insanity.

He is still inside.

Jody Foster is a lesbian.

Allegedly.

TOP TEN CAREERS FOR FAILURES

1. Psychic

Able to predict the future – completely unable to do anything about it. Spend your days subsumed by evil sprites in drafty village halls convincing broken people that their dead relatives actually gave a shit about them.

2. Drummer

A guy who hangs out with musicians...who owns a van...who does not get publishing royalties. Band member most likely to become a plumber.

3. Call centre operative

Hated and reviled by all, no opportunity for career advancement. And it's only a wage slave fill-in job for your real dream, which is...

4. Actor

90% of all actors are unemployed and they still call it show **business**? More deluded still that fame is just around the corner are stand-up comedians.

5. Teacher

Lost the will to live? Failed in every other attempt at what you so laughingly call your life? Then why not consider trying to make yourself heard among a bunch of immoral teenage thugs? You think you'll be the one to make a difference. No. You. Won't.

6. Politician

If you fail as a teacher or gym teacher or businessman or fraudster then either you are

Mark Thatcher or you ought to consider party politics.

7. Farmer

Most common previous occupation of suicides. Once you've counted your EC subsidies, what else is there to enjoy in your stinking sty of a home? Alcohol, mud, isolation? "Piggy give me the come-hither. See, if oi just slip my…? Double barrel shotgun giving oi the come hither…what if oi…?" DOOF!

8. Chugger (Charity mugger)

Excusemehellohaveyougot twominutes...? Have you not noticed that people are swerving to avoid you? That they will not meet your eyes and you will not meet your fucking quota? People do not WANT to sponsor a goat in Africa. You are a lady's part – you useless pile of student toss.

9. Consultant

Park your four wheel drive up in the business park, adjust the Sat Nav and take a good hard look in the rear view mirror. You are earning ridiculous sums for giving spurious advice. How can you live with yourself, you pathetic shell of a man? And you're fat. A fat fucking failure.

10. Publican

Are you an Australian? A former footballer? An alcoholic looking to disguise your problem drinking? Then 18-hour days spent in the nicotine fug and stale beer-reek of broken dreams is the place for you! And one for yourself, squire. Benefits – you are already in the place where all failures gather anyway so how can you fall any further? (See *Farmer.*)

GOD DAMN YOU.... CREATIONS THAT DON'T CUT IT...

Penguins

The point of being a bird is to be able to fly. There are 17 species of penguin in the Antarctic and none of them can get airborne. They walk and swim and the male looks after the eggs. What's the point?

Wasps

The Chav of the insect world. Pointless, ugly and dangerous. Attracted to flapping parents and children with Ribena. Worse than a car boot sale in Eltham.

Deserts

Ooh *sand*. And…more sand. A giant beach with no water.

Mondays

Geldof don't like 'em. We don't like 'em. All God managed on

a Monday was day and night. We don't want daylight when we have a bloody hangover!

Male Pattern Baldness

Not a nice pattern. Who fucks around with their hair every single day of their life? Women. Who loses it? Men. Men in baseball caps.

See also...the appendix, The Isle of Man, PI, market forces and the clitoris.

FAILURE ICON #4
EDDIE "THE EAGLE" EDWARDS

Eddie "The Eagle" Edwards was the UK's first and only Olympic ski jumper. He represented Britain in the 1987 World Championships in Oberstdorf and then again in the 1988 Winter Olympics in Calgary. He came 56th out of

57 competitors. The 57th was disqualified. Eddie's excuse was,

> **"I had no job and no financial support and lived in a country with no snow...where the nearest ski-jumps were a thousand miles away."**

Despite failing to make even the tiniest impression in Olympic terms his failure endeared him to the crowds of people who like to take the piss. Eddie was declared bankrupt in 1992, claiming that a trust fund

designed to handle his earnings wasn't set up properly. He trained in Finland for the 1998 Olympics but failed to qualify. A movie is planned of his life and career. That'll be short then.

FAILURE QUOTE

"It is not enough to succeed. Others must fail."

Gore Vidal

FAILED MOUNTAINEER

Joe Simpson and **Simon Yates** recently attempted to scale the west face of the Silva Grande in the Peruvian Andes. Simpson fell and broke a leg.

Yates thought Simpson was dead and cut the rope joining them. Simpson fell 100 feet, and spent three days crawling

out from a series of ice crevices and caverns. This was later filmed as 'Touching the Void'.

Touching cloth more like.

FAILED PRODUCT
NEW COKE

New Coke replaced *Coca-Cola* in 1985 and was a massive flop. The original formula was reinstated and renamed *Coca-Cola Classic*.

Attempting to change the formula of this teeth-rotting drink upset the American public and pressure group The Old Cola Drinkers of America

lobbied for the formula of Old Coke to be released into the public domain.

After *Classic Coke* was released, the company was accused of setting up the whole thing as a ruse to introduce a new product while reviving interest in the original.

Then Company President, Donald Keough, responded: "Some critics will say Coca-Cola made a marketing

mistake. Some cynics will say that we planned the whole thing. The truth is we are not that dumb, and we are not that smart."

In March 2005 Coke announced a diet product - *Coca-Cola Zero* – which is sweetened with a blend of aspartame and acesulfame potassium. Adverse reactions to aspartame include weight gain, visual impairment, hair loss, irritable bowel, migraine, insomnia, short term

memory problems, arthritis-like stiffness, Obsessive Compulsive Disorder, depression, panic attack, thyroid tumor, memory and speech problems.

Things go better with...what was it again?

FAILURE ICON # 5
PRINCE CHARLES

The Prince of Wales is heir apparent to the throne of England. Charles married Lady Diana Spencer in 1981 in St Paul's Cathedral and had two children, William and (cough) Harry. They divorced in August 1996 after much speculation of affairs on both sides. A year later Diana died in a car crash.

Charles was formally interviewed by Scotland Yard detectives in 2005. Claims of a murder plot were contained in a letter that Diana wrote in which she stated: 'My husband is planning an accident in my car, brake failure and serious head injury to make the path clear for him to marry'.

Charles married his mistress Camilla Parker-Bowles in 2005. He spends his time working for the Prince's Trust, running an

organic farm at Highgrove, shaking hands, doing watercolours, playing polo, asking people how long they have been a tree and waiting to never be King.

FAILED CRIMINALS...

1.

The South African mugger who ran away from a couple he was robbing in Bloemfontein. He ran into a zoo tiger enclosure. He was mauled to death.

2.

The two Australian bandits who posed for CCTV cameras with loot in hand after pulling

off a $130,000 bank heist. They were wearing work badges from the ski shop where they were employed. They got five years.

3.

The two masked gunmen who burst into a house, tied up a woman and two children with duct tape and demanded to know where Joe was. The woman said he didn't live there. Not only did they have the wrong house but the woman's other child had just called the police.

4.

The criminal who ran out of gas and flagged down a police car. Noticing his blood stained clothes, a police search of the car found a dead body.

5.

The car thieves who stole a car from a petrol station and returned an hour later to fill up.

6.

The man from California who was told by his doctor that he could grow cannabis for medical reasons (he had a bad back). After growing about a ton he phoned the sheriff's office to ask if it was legal. Apparently it wasn't.

7.

The robber who evaded police dog and helicopter searches, but who was found the following day hiding under the sheets in his bed.

SPORT FAILURE

In 1960, **Wym Essajas** of Surinam was the first person to be chosen to represent his country in the Olympic 800m. He was told to show up in the afternoon, but the race was in the morning. He missed out and went home.

FAILURE ICON #6
GAZZA

Paul "Gazza" Gascoigne scored 25 goals for Newcastle before being bought by Spurs for £2 million. At Italia '90 he cried after being booked. A knee injury in the 1991 FA Cup Final prevented him from playing for a year. The injuries continued when he moved to Lazio. Returning to the UK he played for Rangers where he

helped win the league table. At Euro 96, Gazza nearly scored against Germany and gave us the waterworks after England lost on penalties. Gazza missed France 98 due to injury and discipline problems and never played for his country again.

Drinking and domestic issues continued to plague him. He lost his contract with Middlesborough, joined Everton, went through rehab and moved

to Burnley. He went on trial for D.C. United but failed to win a contract. He joined Chinese club Gansu Tianma, but left after four games.

In 2004, he announced that he wanted to change his name to "G8".

Huh?

Gascoigne was appointed manager of Portuguese team Algarve United in 2005, but left

to become manager of Kettering Town. He lasted 39 days. A journalist claimed that he was drunk before a match. Gascoigne admitted, "I had a double brandy before the game. Before, it used to be four bottles of whisky. It's not any more." Whay-eye, man.

“If at first you
don’t succeed –
give up.”

ABOUT THE AUTHOR

Marc Blake ticked the box marked 'no publicity' at the start of his career and has had some notable failures since. His BBC producer resigned, a TV company he worked for went bust, one literary agent was murdered and another failed to call him for three years. His novels were optioned for movies but never made, and he was ripped off at the Edinburgh

Fringe Festival to the tune of several thousand pounds. His hit ITV drama resulted in precisely no work and he was forced to sell catalogues for a 'living'. His fifteen year stand up career has so far resulted in no TV deal nor best selling DVD and he is mostly reliant on the 20 mins of love that he is given nightly by audiences all across the UK (before they transfer it to the next performer). His suicide attempts have so far failed...

The Little
Book of

Bling!

ISBN 1-905102-21-6, £2.99

Shag

yourself slim

The most enjoyable way to lose weight

ISBN 1-905102-03-8, £2.99

ISBN 1-905102-17-8, £2.99

ISBN 1-905102-20-8, £2.99

If you enjoyed reading this book and have any comments to make, or suggestions for other Little Books, please email us at: failure@crombiejardine.com.

All our books are available from High Street bookshops, Amazon or Bookpost (P.O. Box 29, Douglas, Isle of Man, IM99 1BQ. Tel: 01624 677237, Fax: 01624 670923, Email: bookshop@enterprise.net. Postage and packing free within the UK).

www.crombiejardine.com